Jesus Comes

The Story of Jesus' Birth
for Children

Written by Ron and Lyn Klug
Illustrated by Paul Konsterlie

Augsburg Publishing House, Minneapolis

Dear Parents:

In all the busy-ness of the Christmas season there is special joy in taking a few quiet moments with a child to share the story of Jesus' birth. This is one way to look beyond the decorations and presents and parties to the meaning of Christmas—that in the birth of Jesus, God entered our history in a special way. In spirit we kneel with our children before the baby in the manger, who is indeed Immanuel, God with us.

While we focus on this story at Christmas, it is a story to be shared all through the year. It reminds us that Jesus' coming is not just an event that occurred long ago in a distant land. Jesus continues to come to us today as we relive his story, hear his Word, sing his praises, and share his love.

Jesus Comes is the first book in a three-book set that tells the life of Jesus for small children. The second book, Jesus Loves, shows Jesus loving people by teaching, feeding, and healing the sick in body and spirit. The third book, Jesus Lives!, tells the story of Jesus' suffering, death, and resurrection, and helps children see how Jesus is alive for us today.

JESUS COMES
The Story of Jesus' Birth for Children

Copyright © 1986 Augsburg Publishing House

LCCC 86-81808   ISBN 0-8066-2234-2

Manufactured in the U.S.A.   APH-10-3497

     5   6   7   8   9   0   1   2   3   4   5   6   7   8   9

Many, many years ago
God's people were waiting.
They had been waiting a long time
for the Savior God had
promised to send.

In a special corner of God's world there lived a young woman named Mary. She loved God and believed that some day God would send the Savior. One day an angel appeared to Mary. "Don't be afraid, Mary," the angel said. "You are going to have a baby —a very special baby—who will be the Savior."

Mary was surprised and puzzled
by the angel's words.
But she said, "God has been good to me.
I will do whatever God wants."

Mary had a friend named Joseph.
He was a carpenter and a good man.
One night God spoke to Joseph in a dream:
"I want you to take Mary as your wife.
She will have a baby,
and you will call him Jesus."

The emperor, a powerful ruler across the sea, decided one day to count all the people in his kingdom. So he ordered everyone to go back to their home towns to be counted.

This meant that Mary and Joseph
had to travel from Nazareth,
where they lived, to the village of Bethlehem.
It was a long, hard journey,
especially for Mary,
who would soon have her baby.

It was late in the day
when Mary and Joseph arrived
in Bethlehem.
They were tired and hungry,
but the village was so crowded with people
that they could find no place to stay.
What would they do? Mary wondered.
Where could the baby be born?

Finally, one innkeeper felt sorry for Mary and Joseph.

"I don't have any room in my house," he said, "but you may stay in my stable with the animals."

There, in the quiet of the night, with the cows and sheep looking on, Jesus was born. Mary wrapped him up to keep him warm and laid him in a manger.

In the hills around Bethlehem shepherds stayed awake all night, guarding their sheep against robbers and wild animals. Suddenly a bright light filled the dark sky.

The shepherds were surprised to see an angel in the sky.
"Don't be afraid," said the angel. "Tonight in Bethlehem the Savior is born."

Suddenly there were many angels. They sang a happy song: "Glory to God, and peace to God's people on earth."

The shepherds hurried to Bethlehem.
There they found the baby Jesus,
just as the angel had said.
They kneeled before him,
filled with joy.

When Jesus was just a few days old,
Mary and Joseph took him to the Temple.
There they thanked God
for the gift of a child.
An old man named Simeon was there.
He took the baby Jesus in his arms
and said, "Lord, you have kept your promise
and sent the Savior. He will
be a light to the whole world."

There was also an old woman named Anna in the Temple. She told everyone she knew about the baby Jesus.

Far, far away in a distant land, some Wise Men searched the sky. One night they saw a bright, new star. "A new king is born," it seemed to say. "Follow me, and I will lead you to him."

For many days the Wise Men traveled
through strange lands, following the star.
Their travels led them to Jerusalem,
to the palace of wicked King Herod.

At the palace they asked King Herod, "Where is the new king who has just been born?"
Herod was worried. A new king? What were these strangers talking about? he wondered.
He called for some of his oldest men, who told him, "The ancient scrolls say that a new king will be born in Bethlehem."

Go to Bethlehem. You will find the new king there," Herod told the Wise Men. "And when you find him, come back and tell me, so I can go see him too." But in his heart King Herod had an evil plan.

The Wise Men left the palace, and again
the special star shone in the sky.
It led them to the house
where Mary and Joseph were now living.

There the Wise Men knelt
and offered Jesus special gifts
—gold and incense and myrrh.

When it was time for the Wise Men to leave,
God told them in a dream, "Don't go back to Herod,
because he has a wicked plan."
So they returned to their land another way.

When King Herod learned
that the Wise Men
had fooled him,
he was very angry.
He ordered his men
to find the newborn king.

God told Joseph in a dream,
"You are in danger.
Take Mary and Jesus and hurry
to the land of Egypt."
Joseph did what God had said.
Mary and Joseph and Jesus
lived in Egypt until it was safe
for them to return home.

Back in their home in Nazareth,
Jesus was happy with Mary and Joseph.
He helped Mary in the house
and worked with Joseph in the carpenter's shop.
He played with his friends.

When Jesus grew up,
he helped many people
by feeding the hungry,
healing the sick,
and teaching them about
the love of God.

Jesus was born almost 2000 years ago
in Bethlehem. Each year we celebrate
his birthday at Christmas.
Like the angels that sang to the shepherds,
we sing songs of joy.
We give one another gifts
that remind us of God's gift of Jesus.

*J*esus came into our world
so many years ago,
yet he still comes to us today.
Jesus comes when we hear the story
of his birth, as you are hearing
it right now.

Jesus comes when we gather with God's people to pray and sing and hear God's Word.

Jesus comes when
we share his love
by helping others.